Ina Mathur

Aria's Whimsical Quest

BookLeaf Publishing

www.bookleafpub.com

Presentation by *BookLeaf Publishing*

Web: www.bookleafpub.com
E-mail: info@bookleafpub.com

ISBN: 9789369545902

First edition 2025

For my loved ones

To Mishika and Aanya,

May you always find the courage to explore new adventures, make wonderful friends, and remember that kindness and laughter can brighten even the quietest moments.

To **Pratul**, my constant source of strength and love, thank you for always believing in me. And to my parents for always supporting and helping me pursue my dreams.

  Aria's Whimsical Quest

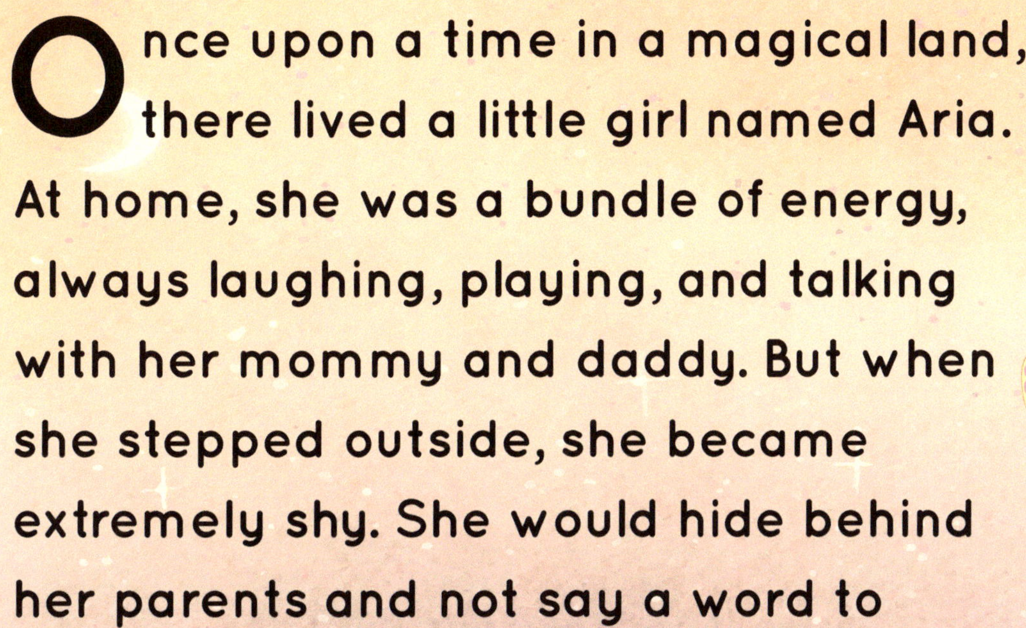

Once upon a time in a magical land, there lived a little girl named Aria. At home, she was a bundle of energy, always laughing, playing, and talking with her mommy and daddy. But when she stepped outside, she became extremely shy. She would hide behind her parents and not say a word to anyone.

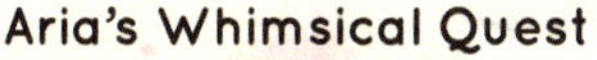

Aria's Whimsical Quest

One sunny day, Aria and her parents decided to visit a beautiful park filled with colorful flowers, towering trees, and friendly animals. As they arrived, Aria clung to her parents, her shyness taking over. She saw other children playing and laughing, but she was too nervous to join in.

Aria's Whimsical Quest

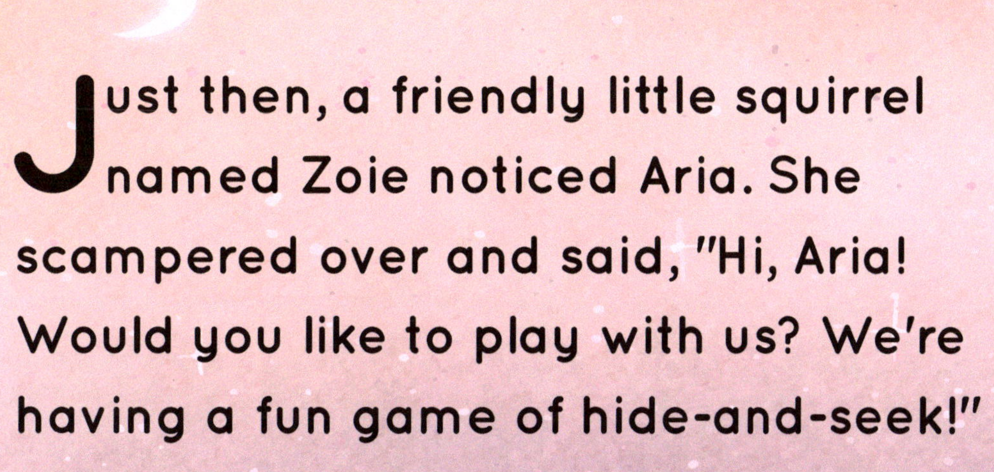

Just then, a friendly little squirrel named Zoie noticed Aria. She scampered over and said, "Hi, Aria! Would you like to play with us? We're having a fun game of hide-and-seek!"

Aria hesitated, looking down at her shoes. She wanted to play, but she was nervous about talking to new people. Zoie noticed her hesitation and said, "It's okay, Aria. We can start together. I'll be with you the whole time!" Zoie's warm smile and the twinkle in her eyes made Aria feel safe, and she found herself nodding slowly.

With Zoie by her side, Aria joined the other children. At first, she stayed close to Zoie, letting him lead the game. But soon, as the other children giggled and cheered her on, Aria began to feel more comfortable. She found herself laughing along with them, her shyness slowly melting away.

   Aria's Whimsical Quest

As they played, Aria realized that the other kids were kind and welcoming. They showed her how to play the game, and soon, she was running around with them, forgetting all about her worries.

    Aria's Whimsical Quest

With time, Aria started talking to more and more people at the park. She discovered that making new friends could be exciting and fun. And whenever she felt shy, she remembered the day she met Zoie and how she helped her come out of her shell.

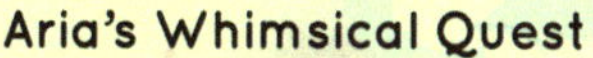

    Aria's Whimsical Quest

From that day on, Aria learned that making new friends and talking to people outside her family could be a joyful adventure. She didn't have to be so shy because there were kind people out there who were ready to welcome her into their circle of friends.

Dear Readers,

Thank you for taking the time to read Aria's journey! Writing this story was a heartfelt experience, as it touches on something many children (and even grown-ups!) face—feeling shy when meeting new people. I believe that with a little kindness and courage, anyone can overcome their fears and discover the joy of making new friends.

I hope Aria's story inspires you to step outside your comfort zone, just as she did, and embrace the adventure of meeting new people. Remember, there's always a friendly Zoie ready to help you along the way.

www.ingramcontent.com/pod-product-compliance
Lightning Source LLC
LaVergne TN
LVHW070046220726
843527LV00029B/481